THE OCTOBERS

A Dissociative Identity Disorder Journal

AVAH RIVERS

THE OCTOBERS

Disclaimer:

All writings in this journal are my own and from my own perspective. Certain names have been changed to protect identity.

Cover by Lara Wynter Designs
Response Artwork by Autumn Marble

> *To all those who suffer, and to those that love them through it.*
>
> *To the God who holds all we will ever need in His capable hands.*

PLEASE READ THIS PAGE CAREFULLY!!!

If **YOU** struggle with Dissociative Identity Disorder, this journal may be a **TRIGGER** for you!!!
Please be sure **you are making safe choices and have support near you if you believe that any of this content may trigger any harmful behaviors!**

This journal is intended for those that struggle as I have to believe that *there is hope*!
You do not struggle alone!
And also, this journal is for my own journey of personal healing as I continue toward my goal of ONE me.

I firmly believe that it is only because of the **grace of God** that I have achieved the incredible amount of healing that I have. I am a very high-functioning individual with DID, and most people would call me quirky and not even realize the truth.

I have learned through hard work, research, perseverance, and self-reflection how to (mostly) maintain a semblance of control over what happens to my mind and to my body as I live with this disorder. It *is* possible, and I pray that within these pages, you may find some healing for yourself.

THE OCTOBERS SPEAK

October demands a voice. Every year, she speaks and I try not to listen. I turn my back and hide behind the walls so readily available, and I think *what I do not remember cannot hurt me.*

This is a lie.

Every year the darkness and the shadows seep through my defenses and grasp at me. So many years of my past they have consumed me.

Now, I have hope. More and more I maintain control of who I am. Of Who speaks. Of Who takes over. Sometimes I allow them to share their stories and I listen. Before, I did not.

This is a journal written by The Octobers.
Their story. My story.
A story of Dissociative Identity Disorder.

Within these pages you will find actual journal entries and other writings, poetry, and my personal thoughts and reflections. There are also pieces of response artwork done by an incredible artist who read our words and created images out of her response to them.

This will not be a chronological journey, but one that I write and put together during the actual month of October, along with writings I have kept since I was young that were done during this difficult month.

This is all of me taking what is typically one of the hardest months of the year and saying IT WILL NOT BE FOR NOTHING.

OCTOBER BREATHES

September 18th, 2019

She has stolen in, early, familiar, taking her spaces, gathering wisps of what is, to become what was.

You don't want her, any of her, but her tears fill your spaces and make them her home. Her pain becomes yours and you cannot let her go. Not like the others. She is yours to protect.

The endless sorrow that she is cries silently, wrenching its dullness deep into your soul. You try to comfort her, to silence her deafening voice. It is not yours to take.

She speaks. Silently. Thunderously. She is everywhere. Nowhere. She is nothing. And yet, she is everything. Her heart beats in synchrony with yours.

The shadows are drawn in softly, a blanket that feels like comfort, but suffocates before you can push it away. It wraps around you, layer upon layer until the heaviness is crushing. No one can hear your muffled pleas.

October breathes. Hiccuping skitters that play along your

veins, sound chords in your head, seep the marrow from your bones. She becomes you. SHE IS YOU.

We do not want her.

I can speak. I barely see, but I will make you hear me. I am your voice, your lies, your heart. You cannot let me go. I am all that you are. The darkness is my home and I am you and we are one and the darkness is the circle of our life.

Hear me cry. I am lost until I am allowed. You will hear me now. I wait, buried, I wait, screaming, I wait, begging, I wait. Give me the voice I seek. I speak so you will hear. Do not push me away.

My tears will drown you. I am there, beneath the waters where they put me, stealing my voice, burying me, flooding me with the pain I scream every second that never ends because no one saves me and you do not listen.

I AM OCTOBER.

There are rainbows, colors that are not really there. Cacophony. There is no stillness. We cannot hear. Run and hide little ones. There is no safety here. Mirror mirror on the wall, mirror mirror who are we all? No voices. No words. No names. We are nothing, no one, nowhere.

Hush, my child, hush. Sleep so you will feel nothing. Nothing. We try.

The mind stretches, a dark sky that settles in its stillness. It is blank and clear. Calm. No winds rage here. No living thing disturbs the emptiness.

I am here. i. 9, 7, 499, all but One, too many we are. we do not exist. it is a lie. you stop s t o p. s t o p st op st op s t o p

---

lower now they speak listen to the voices you seek they have the answers you cannot portray the truth they hold that will lead you to what you do not want to know. walk away

God is all that holds us. I stand there, in His presence. You will not win, any of you, because I am one with Him. I have only the promise He gave me. He loves me. He knows me. He has chosen me. Even as I cry and let you speak and hear your pain, He holds me. He is the One who will save us all.

OF OCTOBERS PAST

A Reflection... **written at the beginning of October, at the start of this project**

The truth was there in front of me as I began this project... all of my journals spread out with a post-it note attached to each cover with each month that contained entries. The realization of truth was shocking. The Octobers had not always been allowed to write.

Journals going back longer than twenty years past gave insight that I was not expecting. March and April months were well populated with entries. For the month's of October, November and December... only *one* entry for each of those months. **One**. My immediate family and I had already determined that those last three months out of every year were the most difficult, but seeing the lack of my own voice through them was startling.

Last year was the first year that I intentionally sat down and allowed The Octobers to write. That entry is titled *October Quicksand*.

This year, in an attempt to diffuse the chaos I was beginning to feel at the end of September, I sat down and allowed my Alter Personalities to write... not knowing that it was The Octobers already seeking a voice. That is the *October Breathes* entry.

Throughout this typically difficult month, I will continue to allow them to write in the hopes that by giving them the voice they seek healing will be found. Reflecting, I wonder if I was too broken in the past to function enough to record the events occurring during the months of Octobers.

Now, **I AM *NOT* BROKEN**. I live. My days are not all lived by one person, but together, we manage to find a place where I can say that great progress has been made. That I know more progress will come.

I can say that, someday, the victory that is already mine will be complete and I will be unified.

SWEET DEATH

Usher in sweet death
To take me from this pain.
For I have called upon you
to become my savior
so that I may not have to bear
the pain of my heart

EXISTENCE

I am screaming but no one can hear me and no is coming to help me and I don't understand how only I know that I feel this way when it is so obvious that I am about to break, that I am holding back tears, that they are burning my throat and eating me alive, and my head is pounding with so much rage that I am about to explode when all I really want to do is lie down and die and forget that I ever existed or that any of you ever existed because I hate all of you and wish that you would all turn inward and look at yourselves and see how horrible you are and how much you have messed me up and screwed with my head and turned me into a fool who cries herself to sleep every night and only wants to die because you have been hurting me for so long that all I can think about are the same self-deprecating thoughts over and over again until I am ready to explode all over all of you so that you will feel my pain and understand what you have done to me and feel sorry and cry because you are so full of ignorance and selfishness that all you can think about are yourselves and how you feel and never mind how I feel as long as you are happy and I am a mess.

FRAYED EDGES

October 3rd, 2019

I am overwhelmed.

Too easily, *it* steals the precarious peace I had grasped. My edges fray. I have tried pushing them back, but their voices rise as my stress level increases. There is nothing I can do to stop the fall once it begins. Only time, and time I do not have. Life steals time.

I pray and I seek my refuge in the moments that are mine.

A quiet few minutes here. Or a momentous small happening that fills me with joy. Like a tear drying, the whispers settle.

Climb into your princess beds my Littles. Hold tight to your Stuffies. Cuddle them close. The pillows are soft. The blankets are warm and welcoming. You are safe. Here, in this room created for you, you are all safe and can rest.

Wait for me there.

I must go to calm the others.

THERAPY

Journal Excerpt: October 17th, 2013

The following is a journal excerpt of the happenings during an October 17th, 2013 therapy appointment, and my thoughts afterward. For the sake of privacy, we will name my therapist Ty.

I had no intention of dealing with anything, but alas, the truth has its own way of coming out.

We were talking about October and her appearance and Ty started talking *to* her (my alter)... telling her it was okay, and that she was safe, and that if she wanted to talk, then Ty was willing to listen.

I remember sipping my whole cup of coffee like a robot while we all stared at Ty and then she (October) said, "Tell her about the lemons."

She wanted Ty to tell *me*.

Ty, of course, said, "No October, you tell me," and boom, I (?) was bent over and I (?) was *there*, saying "*lemons mask the small of death,"* and I (?) was terrified, begging to *not* see, to pretend it was never said.

I saw five or six little girls dancing and there were graves... with bodies in them and I/we were at the house in ——————— of the aunt that used to babysit me (?). *Why just me?*

I don't remember their names or details, but now as I write this I can see the place: the barns, the impression of fields on all sides, *and the big scary barns*. I can feel the fear.

And I see October sitting on a metal slab that pushes into a box in the wall; like a morgue.

I was sobbing.

Begging not to see.

Saying I'd rather not know.

And we never got any further than that one revealing sentence because I cried and cried and cried and then left as soon as I was able to.

And it is too much.

IF THIS IS TRUTH, WILL IT KILL ME?

THE CONSEQUENCE OF THERAPY

...October 23ʳᵈ, 2013...

*There is a story to the lemons and why The Octobers held the secret
disclosed in the therapy appointment on the 17th. I believe that one of
them experienced the trauma.*

*Before that therapy appointment I had been suffering from scent-
induced asthma attacks that had started small and continually gotten
worse, to the point that I was beginning to be afraid to leave my
home. This had been ongoing for years, getting stronger and stronger
with each attack.*

Journal excerpt: October 23, 2013

Someone peels an orange.

I cannot breathe. I go outside to draw in cold air, but I know
the truth now.

I know why I cannot breathe when the scent of citrus
assaults my nostrils. I am having a panic attack. I cannot stop
it. Because I have just learned the truth and it is too fresh.

I am fighting for control when the hostess of the home I am at comes out to ask if I am all right. I tell her the truth. That I am not. She asks if I want her to call my husband and I say no, to call Sylvia. I choose Syliva because she understands how devastating the knowledge is. Because she too suffers from her own hidden memories.

While I wait for Sylvia I tell the hostess all of the truth; about the recovered memory and all of my fears. She listens and does not judge and seems to understand.

I tell her fears I did not know I was struggling with until I voice them.

Backstory: At this time in my journey I had chosen seven people to be my support system because seven is the number of completeness.

I tell her there are only two left.

She tells me that God is only rebuilding my circle.

She is right.

I tell her I am afraid that I will tell the wrong person and the cops will come and get me and put me in the psych ward.

I tell her I'm afraid I will never be whole. That I'll be broken again like last year and I won't have anything to give.

That I mistook my good previous year of somewhat stability as a sign that I could handle this *thing* that I live with, but now I am unsure.

I am grateful to that hostess for speaking life over me after that incident. I did not document her complete response, but I do remember that she prayed over me and told me to not allow the darkness to gain back the hold it had over me from that memory. I had survived then, and I had survived remembering. Now, it was time to heal.

Choosing to surround yourself with people who speak life will aid in your healing.

Choosing those who only serve to reinforce the behaviors, attitudes and negativity of your abusers will only hinder you.

I PRAY *that if you do not have anyone like this in your life that God will send them to you, and that you will recognize them and accept them into your circle of safe people.*

THE END OF THE LEMON ALLERGY

I cannot give you the day or the time.

I *can* tell you that it was so closely linked as to be unmistakable.

Once the memory of the lemons was spoken, it lost its power.

Yes, I reacted **once** after the truth was out. That was a stronghold trying to gain back its hold.

I refused. I allowed God to fill that horrible memory with the truth and His amazing grace so that I could heal from it.

Since then, I have not reacted to the scent of lemons or oranges. I also can drink orange juice, something I could not do when the symptoms were only explainable as some form of 'allergy.'

MEMORY is linked to our five senses. Scent is one of them, and the most powerful of them all, according to research.

DESCEND

I gather

inside of myself

Becoming heavy

A weight that pulls

Stretches

Drifts away from the core of me

Down

a trembling gravity

I fall

to explode into fragments

that will dry into nothing

THE FOG

October 7, 2019

It's a quiet humming. In my center. It hurts. I am afraid of it.

Sharp prickles dig into my cells, fangs that take hold, bodies that curl warm and cold around them and make them their own. It is safe when they live outside. Once they are inside, the weight of them shrouds me in fog and I am lost.

Behind the fog, I cannot speak. They speak. I watch. I know that I am there, but I am not. They are there.

Now, I hear them. Before I would have only the empty time to tell me they were out. Living, or not living, whatever each of them does.

Now, there is the fog. Walls that surround me.

Tears press hard, threatening storms that I try to hold back. If I let them fall I will lose control. I don't want this. I want my peace. I want the calm. Why is it so fleeting? So hard to hold onto?

I can't explain any of this. How do you tell what you do not understand yourself? This isn't me. I don't even know if there is a me. What is mine and mine alone? NOTHING. I am scattered in the air like feathers that float and never find a place to rest upon the ground.

Drifting, always drifting, aloft upon the whims of the breezes that carry the emotions that triggers the deep places that open to live. But none of it is life. *THIS IS NOT LIFE.*

Still, I do not crave yours. Your insecurities, your complaints about health and home and friends and money. I allow mine to rule only for a time. Then I give them away and let another rise. To express views and thoughts and opinions that may not be shared with us all.

- I like green.
- They like floral.
- I like coffee. A LOT.
- Some of them like tea.
- I dislike Hallmark.
- A small number of them thrive on the shallowness of love.

IT DOESN'T MATTER WHAT THEY LIKE OR DO NOT LIKE.

Tomorrow, it will Change. Tomorrow I will Change.

Always, change. That is why we hate it.

CHANGE means something is wrong. That our safe world is disrupted. One place. One person. One sound. One color. One thought. ONE. That is a number we hardly ever believe in.

EMPTY SCREAMS

I scream; the world is black
it tilts,
does not right itself.
My breath is lost,
my body numb
The screams subside and leave me _{broken}

JOURNAL ENTRY

Wednesday the 17th, 2008

Panicky all day, got worse before I left. I requested a vacation day in case it got worse.

Husband kept asking if I was all right. I kept saying fine. Didn't want to deal with kids, didn't want him around.

Highly irritable.

Thursday the 18th, 2008

Next AM I felt okay, but decided not to go to work just in case. Spent entire day adding songs to I-Tunes (relaxing music). Felt better.

Friday the 19th, 2008

Feel odd. A little panicky. Cannot breathe. Worried about stuff. Warning sign—I am skipping things I have to do.

IN MAY OF 2008, at work, I walked out onto the third story stairwell and looked over the railing and decided that I was finished. I would jump. I could handle no more.

I worked in a company that had a nurse on staff, and who was also my boss, and I remember telling myself that if I walked to her desk and she was not there, that I was going to jump.

God was watching out for me that day, because it was not often that she was at her desk. At that moment, at that time, she was, and she asked me what was wrong, and I began to cry. My memory is fuzzy at this point, but she took me into an empty conference room for a long time, and at the end of it, she pulled another employee to drive me to the hospital with specific instructions that she was not to leave me until I was admitted.

I was admitted into the psych ward, where I spent a week.

I remember that I wanted to die for the first few days. I remember that I was angry that they wouldn't allow me more than one tiny styrofoam cup of coffee in the morning. I remember thinking that everyone else there was crazy and that I didn't belong there.

I painted a rug during craft time that I still have from those days. It reminds me of how far I have come since then.

I was given a lot of labels over years. Bipolar. Borderline Personality Disorder. Clinically Depressed. It didn't matter. None of the medications were dealing with the root issue.

After release from the hospital, I was on a strict regimen of medications and counseling sessions. That day the ended with me in the hospital was a catalyst into several frightening years of horrible memories. I battled with suicidal tendencies, cutting, and oppressing darkness.

THERE WERE MORE THAN ONE OF ME.

I refused the diagnosis of Dissociative Identity Disorder. At that time, I was still in denial. Still fighting the truth. I had decades of therapy, dating back to when I was fifteen, I believe, and many, many of my therapists tried to gently suggest the truth. I didn't want it.

This is something you never want.

Those journal entries were many months after that week in the hospital. It was a very, very slow progressive journey. There were many, many days that I did not think I would make it through until morning.

By the grace of God, and the plan He had for me, I am here to speak.

I made it through the years full of suffering and trauma, caused by suffering and trauma.

I chose to slowly begin to accept the truth, to learn my triggers, and to heal.

I wanted something more. Always, I had prayed for it. Even if I didn't understand it. **LIFE.**

I have regrets. That I did not heal sooner is one of them. Truthfully, I am not sure it was possible. Looking back, my regrets are founded in what was lost.

However, I am grateful that I can live now, even though it is not perfect yet.

I am happy. I am content.

There are bad days. But there are so many less than what there used to be.

Before, it was bad years. Not days.

Before, it was bad months. Not days.

I'll take days.

And one day, those days may not have memories, or triggers, or trauma involved.

They'll just be days that don't go as planned because life is life.

THE TRUTH

Wildly I erupt in panic, tears falling, breath catching, the burning core of who I am torn into two as I see what cannot be true. Blinking rapidly, I pant, blink, pant, blink, each time expecting, each time terrified that something will change. NOTHING CHANGES.

What words, what thoughts, what answer can explain the rend in reality that has broken my mind, fractured my soul, opened up my body so another can inhabit its space?

I scream at those eyes, plead with myself to acknowledge that nothing is wrong, that I am only having a temporary break from my sanity, sobbing when I look back caustically at myself, tears on my fingers betraying the lie on my face.

A blubbering, frightened child.

A restrained acerbic stranger.

I cannot tell, I must hold my secret close. I am afraid that they will tell me what I already know; I am crazy. They will lock me up, take me away from my home, strip me of what sanity I have left.

So I must live. I must pretend. I must hide the eyes that are not mine, hide the identity that threatens to steal mine, become exactly who they expect me to be.

I MUST BELIEVE THE LIE.

WHO ARE YOU?

Once I was by myself. I reached out and found
everyone I needed so that I wasn't. Strong enough
to live. Broken enough to die.

I don't know who they are. They know, somewhere inside. I don't think I ever wanted to know or to understand. No one was given names because it was easier not to slip. Stay, I said. That's all you need to do.

No one lived.

No one died.

They just fell apart because they were never whole to begin with. Fragments meant to become something great, but who became nothing at all.

Dreams never realized. Personalities never materialized. Pieces created that fell through the cracks and got lost.

What did they do? I don't know.

WHO ARE THEY? I DON'T KNOW.

I don't remember creating any of them. I hear them speak and I still want to deny. I feel them when they take hold and do what I apparently created them to do, and I deny. I act in ways that I see and hear that I know are not me, and again, *I do not believe*.

THAT IS EXACTLY THE POINT.

Do not see. Do not hear. Do not know. Deny everything.

None of it is real. Nothing happened.

I am mistaken.

Charlene is the one who lies

Cassandra is really real

Olivia tells lies

The room for the princesses is the first real home we have ever known.

IT IS SAFE.

Do you feel us when you let us speak? How do you deny?

All of use are real,

more real than you

you are the illusion

when you fall in, then — there the darkness will crawl over you and you will die

we all died

you put us in boxes like they did to you

we died because you killed us

we want to live

this is our time... that is why you fight so hard because we want to reach the surface and feel what you do not

it is what we know

we will rip you apart

> *no*
> *live*
> *you are in control*
> *you choose*
> *they are the broken ones*
> *those voices are October*
> *i will protect you*
> *that is my job*
> *they have no power unless you give it*

Alaina.

... A reflection while writing the above, written after the entry was finished...

I see the words I let them write and they are blurry, like I see out of multiple eyes. My head hurts. I keep waiting for the words to correct themselves, but they do not. I am calm. Strangely so, as the experience of allowing what they say to come out onto the page should be terrify-

ing. How do you deny what is so weird? When you write that and they say, "we are not weird," in your head?

OCTOBER IS GOING TO BE A VERY LONG
MONTH.

I need to sleep now. So they will rest. So I can take back my mind.

A PRAYER

A sea of fear rising up
Sharp teeth bared to bite
I reach up to the Heavens
Begging for strength to fight

His heart awaits with open arms
Ready for my plea
His embrace wraps me in His comfort
And His love pours over me

I beg of Him
Don't let go
I need you Jesus
Let your peace flow

SNIPPETS...

—scribblings from my writings that I wrote throughout my earlier years

I search for the door that will lock you away, drown out your cries and pleas that you weep.

Halfway through the night you awake me with your screams, but then I realize that they are mine.

Regressing back to when the screams were real,

back to what you forgot and still only have pieces of.

Your body takes on its own mind, kicking and flailing, trying to push away the demons that haunt.

Claws are reaching out to tear me apart.

It's like a black hole opening to swallow me.

I am helpless to prevent it.

I can almost feel the shadows choking my brain, blinding me to everything but pain.

I want to run, but I have nowhere to go.

There is no safe haven.

I have no one.

SNIPPETS CONTINUED...

Broken pieces of my heart lay scattered on the floor.

They sparkle like tears that no one wiped away.

My fingers bleed from their efforts to piece my heart back together,
shredded by the battles my heart has fought and lost.

The fragments are crumbling, too abused to go on.

I am left with only half of a heart, too torn to cry anymore.

My emotions quiver. They see the shadows that flit through my head.

I fight the pain within, reaching out for help.

I scream at their worthless words even as I hold on to hope.

Their frustration hurts me more,

They don't know how to save me.

Words will not leave my mouth, only helpless little whimpers.

Their tears anger me.

Why can they not understand?

I am lost inside of this black bubble, wishing that they would see.

MORE SNIPPETS...

The mist cries out to be parted, to free my tortured mind.

It struggles for one gasp of breath,
one blink to escape, to be blind.

It shares its home with trembling darkness, unspoken, unknown fears.

Long fingers of silence grip tightly,
squeezing out memories in tears.

The victim of a forgotten past.

Only the mind aware, afraid to tell.

Secrets that were told to forever last.

Closer to the surface they rise and grasp,
loosening into her dreams.

Terror takes everything she is.

Lost in the silence, her mind echoing with their screams.

I am captivated as the world flows around me and past me.

I feel the blood in my veins, like wild fire. I watch, but I am frustrated, unable to do anything.

Inside of me, I can feel the anger. I cry but I do not cry. It gnaws at me.

Waves of pain crush me, close in around me like a tide pulling me deep until I have no hope of reaching the surface.

Strange and unknown visions rise up, lost memories.

I shove them aside in panic, into the water, letting them be sucked away in the current.

I TURN MY FACE AWAY FROM THE WORLD.

FACING THE DAY

October 9th, 2019

IT IS TOO MUCH.

I cannot pretend the swirling is calm. A whirlwind spins, angry, pulling in my breath, gathering the bits of peace and joy and presence that I had gained.

I get up but everything in me tells me to stay buried beneath the covers where it is safe.

I get ready, but I am not. The day sharpens its knife with glee.

I will go through the motions as I have taught myself to do, but inside I know too well the chaos and despair and pain and fear that wraps around my neck and suffocates with every breath.

I am unable to turn away. Life forces you to live it.

I stroke my fingers over the softness of a blanket as I walk by, yearning for what it offers.

Time is my enemy.

The Octobers always fight it. They require so much.

Every year they are denied and their tears are all I hear as the days grow darker and harder, and remind us all why we are RIPPED TO PIECES.

REPRESSED

It is a dream that comes often,

one that is not so easily forgotten.

It is full of shadows that grip and haunt and reach out to suck all coherence from the mind to leave it in tatters.

The fingers pull painfully at memories buried deep enough to die

persistently urging them to arise and let the truth be known.

It is a battle that must be fought.

It will grow stronger until the subconscious can no longer hold onto the scraps that hold the pain locked away.

With the truth

will come the answers

we have searched for all this time

but DON'T WANT TO KNOW.

THE MIRROR

I would guess that it is normal for those like me to avoid the mirror.

We do not wish to see what we already know.

The differences that define our reality to our own eyes. The shape we are, the age, the eyes. Always, the eyes are the ones I look away from.

For the longest time, I thought that perhaps I was possessed. Except one who is SAVED by the blood of Christ cannot be possessed.

Still, I would see, and I would know, that it was not me that looked back at me from my reflection.

A terrifying reality that tears at the mind and makes one question their own sanity.

The vision of me lives like a slap in my mind

laughing and taunting me,
sometimes crying and begging for things I do not want to give
I strive to be what it tells me I should,
to turn away when what it wants is wrong.
Sometimes I think I would be better if I could only listen.
Just out of reach, the eyes mock me, silently beseeching.
The glittering hatred of the mirror is my enemy.
I see the monster.
I cannot make her go away.
I barter with her voice,
I curse at the image,
at the one WHO IS ME.
I hate her.
I see her rage. It is mine.
My eyes are in the reflection, but they are not mine.

I see this common theme throughout much of my writing.

I struggle with it almost daily. I have taken many steps to make the differences as subtle as possible. Still, sometimes I am younger than I am.

I reach for certain colors or patterns. I only wear black. Then color.

I take on favorite shoes for months, and then I hate them.

I adore a pair of earrings, then they are tossed aside for months until I remember that I love them again.

I wear glasses. And then I do not.

I am overweight and only wear boyfriend jeans to hide it. And then I see that I am skinny and only wear my skinny jeans again.

I stare at the clothes in my closet and know that they are nice clothes. Trendy and cute. Inviting. They only make me want to cry. THEY DO NOT ALLOW ME TO HIDE.

It is with relief that I find a baggy pair of jeans and a sweatshirt. But then, always, there is the battle over shoes. We do not like socks. Hardly any of us. But there are rules even for the ones that want to hide. Your shoes must match.

And then, after all of that, do not look in the mirror... or you will have to start all over.

BEGINNING AGAIN

Rose colored glasses are broken at my feet,

shattered by illusions.

Walls tumble and fall.

I stand in their rubbish, feeling stripped and beaten.

All I knew is lost, and I must begin again...

vulnerable and barren.

A battle rises up, raging and fierce.

I refuse to accept.

I deny the truth that stares me in the face.

I am unwilling to open my heart, to let my feelings flow and to be free.

Was what I felt before horribly misplaced?

The past has opened its door and emptied its excuses.

My bad voice quarrels with its counterpart,

seeking favor in my unaware eyes.

ONE fights to close my heart.

The OTHER to open it.

NIGHT

the eyes **close**

they hardly ever see

the **dark** is the safest place to be

closed why do you not hear me except when **darkness** falls

stop talking you fools

hold closed the doors

the **darkness** hides what does not need to be seen

they took it from me

my peace

who i was

i have never been whole

from the moment you didn't want me you cursed me

i no longer cry

or maybe i do where no one hears

i can hear

when it is **DARK**

Only There the Truth can be Seen

FORGOTTEN

Oct 2019

I have forgotten people.

People that I loved. Who I spent lots of time with over spans of years. Forgotten.

One of me loved them. For whatever reason, as my healing progressed and alters merged and were able to say good-bye, their friends and habits were lost. Forgotten.

It wasn't purposeful. Honestly, it was awkward. To know you are supposed to love someone and be close but you don't know why and can't figure out how to connect anymore.

How do you look into someones eyes and know things about them, but what used to make you click is gone, and so you see nothing and your heart is asking what you are doing, but your mind tells you to stay and listen and to react... but you feel nothing?

I am sorry. But the word is empty, because the emotion behind it is lacking. There are so many that I have forgotten.

Forgetting is the definition of what I am. I created myself to forget. How can you be sorry when you simply do what you taught yourself to do to survive?

How deep would I have to dig to no longer forget? What horrors would I find? Why would I want to?

Over and over I ask these questions. I don't want to remember. Healing is remembering. Maybe not all of it. I believe that God knows what I need to recall and what I do not. Some things I am unsure I will ever be able to handle and He holds those memories for me.

Others, I must remember. To realize that I am safe now. To know that I survived. To recognize the trigger so it no longer causes the switch created to protect me from it.

Forgetting is the blessing. And the curse. Some things I must not forget. Others I pray to forget. If I have forgotten you, then please understand it was never really me. For whatever reason, you were chosen by God to guide me through a season.

I have no choice but to trust that the outcome of that season ended as it was meant to. Somewhere, buried deep in my heart where the merged ones sleep forever now, you are there. Cherished. The memories of you held close.

FORGIVE ME FOR FORGETTING.

FACEBOOK... POST AT YOUR OWN RISK...

A record of Facebook posts that reflect inner turmoil and the life that I live:

Oct 8th, 2009

It shines like freedom; it blinds me. Tears fall red.

Oct 8th, 2009

Back story: At one time, one or more of my alters suffered from bipolar disorder. Those alters have now merged and I have not suffered from the disorder since. It has been years.

Fine. I'm fine. I'm bipolar. So fine means I am as good as it's gonna get until the fine goes back on an upswing to happy again. K? I AM FINE. I got through the last episodes. I'll get through this one. So if I don't FEEL like talking it's probably because it's better that I don't talk to you. So you should just thank me for ignoring all of you who keep asking me if I am OK. K? I.m.f.i.n.e.

Oct 12, 2009

Weird. I drank 5 glasses of milk with dinner. I don't even like milk.

Oct 19, 2009

I don't understand why when people see my name on the chat list they don't want to chat with me. Seriously, I am very interesting, you know.

Oct 20, 2009

Why doesn't God just come back and end it already? I'm tired of being here.

Oct 20, 2009

Do I really care? Right now, I really just don't. Sorry.

Oct 30, 2013

ONE. MORE. DAY. OF OCTOBER. GOOD RIDDANCE!!

Oct 14, 2014

October is so annoying. On a bright note, it's going waaaaay better than last year.

Oct 27, 2014

I'm not scared, 'cause really, if it gets me, I'm going somewhere better... somewhere I've wanted to go for a long time.

Oct 27, 2014

I'm emotionally drained right now. If you need me, I don't have anything to give you but prayer. I am praying for you... and waiting until I can do more. ——————— Love me through it like you always do and when my capacity increases, I know you'll welcome me back with open arms.

#behonestaboutwhereyouare

#stopthelies

IDENTITY

October 10th, 2019

This is madness.

These endeavors that we have taken on.

In this month.

I AM CRAZY.

It is a challenge. To myself. Unnecessary? Or so much more? Perhaps the key to October is filling my days. Letting them delve into what is offered and to embrace it.

I printed out everything to put this all together and was startled by entries that I do not remember writing. I know that I am doing this, but still, each time another entry appears I cannot help my surprise.

Who are they that speak? What is their purpose?

They do not tell *me*.

I have heard stories of others who struggle with this disorder.

They are different. I have never found one that has made me feel as though I share my own experiences.

That knowledge feeds my denial. If I am not the same, then I cannot be what they are.

But I am. I have heard them speak. Looked into their faces. Felt their pain. Remembered their trauma.

Yes darling Cheetos girl, I hear you now. (this will make sense later)

They talk to me as I write. They want me to hear sometimes. To know they exist. I never know if it is a taunt or encouragement.

Is it wrong to find all of this fascinating? To realize the complexities of the mind that God gave us? How can a part of someone die so that another rises up to live? Not one, but many?

Satan must have laughed with glee when he used trauma to murder Gods people. But God said no, and gave us a way to live.

I LIVE THIS WAY.

Once, I did not understand why God would allow such trauma in my life. Why would he allow so much pain and hurt to take over everything that I was, so that I wished only to die every second of every day?

Now, I am grateful. Grateful.

NOT for the pain and the trauma, but for what it has made me.

I am not whole. But I am no longer broken. For moments, I

might believe that I am. Or days. Perhaps even a week. But now, I know that I will find myself again and I will be okay.

LIVING THIS WAY has ironically taught me identity.

What an odd thing from someone who literally has so many?

Do you understand?

I have more identity than most of the people I know. Even if there are hundreds of them.

The ONE who I am created to be knows who she is. Who she loves. What she believes. What she is worth.

I am a child of God.
He is my savior, my grace, my healer.
I am nothing without Him who holds every
second of my day in His hands.

THE CHEETO'S ENTRY

...because The Octobers wrote to her I am including this.

My husband found a podcast done by a woman who suffers with DID. In one episode, she speaks of a notebook that she and her alters use to communicate with each other. My husband thought this was a great idea. Me, not so much. Still, after awhile, I put one next to a chair just to see what would happen.

Entry:

I am Ceville.

I am not you.

Your Cheetos are good.

I peruse. I see. I make sure where you are is safe.

I am not out often.

You have laundry to fold, and an email to answer. I do not do those things. I think all I do is see.

Thank you for the Cheetos.

Oh. I am... I do not know how old I am, apparently. I cannot recall.

The very next entry, in completely different handwriting:

Stop eating the Cheetos.

They will make you fat and they are gross and we don't like them.

Seriously, stop. Okay?

UNENDING FIELD

What field is this that stretches far?

The pebbled dirt the path we take, buried deep beneath the dying grass.

Particles spread like dry ash, we meld within the layers. No form, no substance, hollow cores opening wide for suffocating sand to fill us and give shape to something real.

Moved by trembling. Crushed with every step.

Losing parts of our self upon the whim of the breeze.

Carried away and crying out for the piece that was lost even though we fear what it held.

An hourglass empty.

Where is what is meant to be there? This emptiness is all I feel, all I know.

How can I care when your words fall and drain away as though they were never there?

The darkness shimmers behind my eyes.

A world of nothing.

Flat earth that goes on forever.

No flower of grace.

No pool of peace. No tree of praise.

No creature of warmth.

My moments are those when I force myself to feel what is beneath my fingers. The softness of a blanket. The hard wood of the table. The roughness of my jeans.

There is nothing given in return. A grounding that confuses what is not solidified.

Alone I stand. The field chases the horizon. There is only that, so far away.

Unreachable.

It is better to be the pebbles in the dirt.

CHAOS

Our voice was taken away.

I have given it back.

I am too many people. Too many unfamiliar emotions and ages and feelings that I do not like but cannot separate from.

They are ridiculous. It is fun for them because they have never lived.

IT IS NOT FUN FOR ME.

It isn't what they want to hear, but it is like corralling a herd of wild mustangs who do not care about the rules.

THE SIGNIFICANCE OF EVERYTHING

October 22nd, 2019

I am frantic in my mind.

My problems are catching up with me, clawing at my back and making me feel unsettled and like bad things are going to happen.

It's usually my fault. Sometimes I believe so wholeheartedly that everything will be fine that I make choices that seem like they aren't going to cause trouble, but in the end they do.

Nothing big. It's never anything big or life-changing. Simple things are usually the hardest. I either don't understand them or they become so momentous that I can't handle them at all.

It's amazing how much trouble a simple thing can cause. For example, not eating starts to become such a habit that you don't even feel hunger anymore and it becomes common to not eat until six in the evening every day. Then later and later until you realize you never ate at all.

Drinking water. It's required. Healthy. Except it is boring and doesn't taste good. So you don't drink it and you think, maybe tomorrow, and then it's been a week or longer and you know you are dehydrated but it just seems so insignificant and huge at the same time that you still don't drink any, even though you can see the consequences on your skin and your urine is so dark it's all but screaming at you.

One pile on the table becomes three, and then the table is covered and putting it all away is overwhelming and you just don't because it will all probably end up right back on the table again anyway.

Small things. Except they aren't.

My child says "You had a cleaner out," when I do clean.

My brain tells me I have an alter out when I have to have French fries and only French fries are going to make me happy and nothing else.

Or I have to wear an orange shirt and even though that is ridiculous, the pink shirt I put on comes off, and then so does the striped one, and the sweater, and the one I liked last week but I hate it now. Only the orange shirt makes us all feel prepared and put together.

IT'S EXHAUSTING. I AM SO TIRED. I CAN'T KEEP UP.

OUTSIDE THE WALL

I feel battered.

Like pieces of me are falling out and I cannot find them. The world spins around me but all I see is the wall in front of me. It is foggy. A shield that separates me from everything... almost...

—there are people who need things from me that I do not want to give.

I don't wish to speak or engage with most of them. How does one work when they are like me? How do they survive?

I want to turn away. To leave. To find some place quiet and that is comforting.

Alone.

> *Please leave me alone.*
> *It is the only safe place.*

OCTOBER QUICKSAND

October 2018

Too many times she'd been sucked in by the trauma of her past. It pulled at her core and clawed at her insides every time she managed to erect a wall around her that gave her the illusion her life was livable. Like quicksand, one part of her would sink in and the harder she tried to shake it off, the more she drowned in it, until it consumed her normalcy, her illusion, her lie, and pulled her deep into the depths of suffocating blackness.

One little whisper in October. Words she didn't even understand. A shadow that didn't exist, but was there behind her as real as the beating of her heart. A twitch of pain in her head that felt like her eyes were being pulled back so something, or someone else, could look out. And always, the whispers that multiplied until the pain in her head never dulled.

October.

Hell month.

Demons parading around and dancing with the night. Raging with lust for souls that feed themselves to the devil. Clinging to souls that don't see them, ignorance a blissful dessert.

The month most of the world welcomes evil.

They shriek, they taunt, they torment, they whisper.

That was her truth. The line between the worlds.

Life was the lie.

A society of people rushing through life, drinking to be numb on weekends, swearing at drivers on the way to work on the weekdays, checking Facebook every hour like clockwork, stressing over what to make for dinner.

Not her life.

She didn't want it anyway, but if she had a choice, she would choose their lives.

Only in October. October was like a game. Every year, it would start and she would think, "I'll be ok."

A day would pass. Two. Maybe more. Then the whispers.

Denial would raise it's head proudly and give back a day.

Another whisper. The shadow. The twitch in her eye. The pain.

The lie she lived every day would raise its ugly head; SHE'D NEVER BEEN NORMAL. Never been ok. Never really lived.

She'd only been surviving since birth, running from what had been done to her.

Illusions shattered leave broken pieces to put back

together, but the cracks remain.

The threat of falling to pieces again with no glue strong enough to never break again.

The darkness calls her name when the sun disappears each night. Stronger with each passing day. Shorter days, longer nights for the demons to dance. Chanting the whispers that invade her head, tear her apart from the inside; QUICKSAND.

She sinks the more she struggles not to.

The fear that overtakes her wins because she can't overcome, can't find peace, hears no answers to her prayers.

There is no peace. No freedom.

Every year that passes she wonders how she still lives. Wonders how when October passes, she sobs on solid ground with quicksand still clinging to her limbs, still coating her lungs, deep under her fingernails.

She remembers the years past every day that the whispers taunt her. Remembers the pain, the struggle, the darkness.

She dreams of death, wishes for it, prays for it, begs for it.

You could ask her, but she won't know how to tell you what happens inside of her head. Isn't able to comprehend the madness herself.

If she can't face the truth, what good are those who reach out to try and help?

The truant inside speaks to her. Buried deep, her other selves hide in fear. Call for her to please hide with them.

Don't see.

Don't remember.

Don't live.

Only death can bring freedom. There is no life as long as the secrets live. There is no life if she never faces them and defeats them.

She doesn't want to know. She tries to. Tries to understand, spends hours searching for what eludes her. What causes the pain?

How can truth that causes such pain hide? Truth could destroy her if she finds it, but she searches anyway, BECAUSE SHE IS ALREADY DESTROYED.

The demons dance and parade in the streets.

They shine from the eyes that look into hers.

Run like children everywhere she goes.

They fill the sky with darkness.

Rise up on lawns like beacons.

Follow her.

Are all over her.

Are in her head.

She tries to separate them out. They feel at home. Like decor that does not belong she tries to tear them out, to lock them out, to seal every hole they find.

She cries. They feed off of her tears. Their nails are sharp, their ways wily, their souls evil.

They seek out the places they have known in her past that she cannot see, they whisper to her, scrape their long, decaying nails along her skin as she sleeps, filling her dreams with terror.

She sleeps to find peace, exhausted from the ongoing battle, but they weave into her dreams, eat away at her soul, and she awakes with a pounding heart, knowing today is yet another she cannot seem to change, though she will try, and fail.

Others see her as odd, call her quirky, accept that she is and always has been different, even if they don't understand why.

The idiosyncrasies that make her a whole to them are the parts that scream at her from the darkness.

The parts created to cope, to defend, to live.

A soul torn into pieces by horrific trauma, battered to mold together by nothing more than the body that walks, a tomb of terrified selves that all are one, that rise up to the surface when a spark of life emits a trigger that calls their names and unwittingly causes them to look up and see what comes for them.

It is darkness, nights full of moons hidden by mists that lend light to secret betrayals of all that is good, and fills the earth with innocent blood that seeps down into the core of the universe.

The night of evil rises, one she hides from every year, holed up in her safe haven to ward off the pressing taunt of something she knows lives deep inside of her without her permission, something that she cannot cleanse.

She waits and trembles and finally sleeps, the last night of Hell month seeping away AS SHE LIVES STILL.

And she awakes to November.

ABOUT THE AUTHOR

Avah Rivers lives a somewhat normal life in a smallish town with her family. She has two cats that she adores, a closet full of clothes that mostly she doesn't like (even though they are super cute), and a colorful array of Yeti's for her endless supply of coffee.

She is one of those weird writers who feel like the reader when she writes. Without an outline (because who could possibly contain all of that information between so many people sharing the space in her head), she sits down to write and giggles and ooh's and aah's over the plot twists that come out as she writes. Sometimes, in Panera, she gets some odd looks.

This journal is her delve into non-fiction, and while she finds releasing such personal details of her life into the world intimidating, she also finds the writings to be fascinating as she is not typically the one writing them, and so there is little emotion attached to releasing them.

ACKNOWLEDGMENTS

This battle is one that is never fought alone.

I am so blessed by the man who has stood by my side for many, many hard years of marriage that have become mostly peaceful and, and perhaps, somewhat normal.

I love you so deeply.

You have fought so hard to become my rock. A stable point that never moves, despite the waves that consistently beat away at the stone.

By the grace that God has given to us, together, we have created a beautiful testimony of perseverance. A message that gives credence to the vows we spoke to one another.

> *...to have and to hold from this day forward. For better or for worse, for richer, for poorer, in sickness and in health, to love and to cherish, till death do us part, according to God's holy law; and this is my solemn vow.*
>
> *Amen*